What in my head is going on?

Start here:

Has life changed for you recently?

Oh, things have to change again?

Is there something or someone you miss?

Are you sad because of something that happened?

It's totally normal to have all kinds of unusual feelings during these times.

Giving a name to our feelings can help us recognize what is going on in our head.

Let's see if we can name some of these emotions.

Denial

Definition: Saying that something is not true. Refusing to accept or believe someone or something.

When we experience loss or something important in our life is changing, we might start with saying it's not true.

No, it won't happen to me. I never get sick.

I can't believe it! Wear a mask for protection? NO WAY! Besides, what will my friends say...

...if they see me wearing this silly looking thing?

Anger

Definition: a strong feeling of displeasure. Angry feelings can range from being annoyed to extreme rage.

Once we see that it's for real, we might get angry about it.

What? We can't go to the pizza parlor?

I want to go to my sports game, NOW!

Will I still get to lick your plate for leftovers?

"That's not fair. Why is this happening to me?"

"Hey, your piece is bigger than mine. THAT'S not fair!"

We might even try and blame someone.

"It's YOUR fault."

Bargaining

Definition: to discuss the terms of something. To negotiate details to our favor.

We might try offering something in exchange to avoid the loss.

Example: If you do this, then I'll do that.

If I don't touch anything, can we still go to the pizza parlor? PLEASE?

Meaning

Definition: feeling determined to do or achieve something, finding purpose and a goal.

And lastly, we might find a goal that helps us overcome the loss even better.

For example, helping others is one way to find meaning and purpose.

"We could also make extra pizza for the neighbors."

Do you remember having some of these feelings?

YES!

YESS!!

MEOWYES!

Not everyone goes through these feelings in that order.

Sometimes we even bounce between them a few times.

Physical Symptoms
Sometimes these feelings may have physical symptoms or signs.

When going through a difficult time, we have days when we feel good and days when we don't.

March 20, 2020

March 25, 2020

March 30, 2020

Just remember that your feelings are as unique as you are.

And... the GOOD NEWS is that in time the good days...

1	2	3
NO WAY!	Got upset at Teddy.	Had a rough day.
7	**8**	**9**
Ate in peace.	Did some research.	Tried on a mask
13	14	15

Notes:

...will begin to outnumber the bad days.
WHAT'S YOUR HAPPY ENDING?

www.kidible.eu

Published by iCharacter Limited ®. (Ireland)
Kidible ® is an imprint of iCharacter Limited.
By Agnes and Salem de Bezenac
Illustrated by Agnes de Bezenac
Colored by Adinade Bezenac
Copyright 2020. All rights reserved.

Visit our website www.kidible.eu for more great kids books and downloads.

Copyright © 2020 by iCharacter Limited ®. All rights reserved. No part of this book may be reproduced in any form or by any electronic or mechanical means, including information storage and retrieval systems, without written permission from the publisher or author, except in the case of a reviewer, who may quote brief passages embodied in critical articles or in a review.

The 6 stages of grief poster

Agnes de Bezenac

1 Denial

2 Anger

3 Bargaining

4 Depression

5 Acceptance

6 Meaning

www.ingramcontent.com/pod-product-compliance
Lightning Source LLC
Chambersburg PA
CBHW061811070526
44586CB00024B/2805